AF602063

Standard Copyright Page (Children's Picture Book)

The Place We Call Home
Raising "soft citizens" in the Champlain Adirondack Biosphere Reserve

First edition

Published by Shared Ground Press
Central New York, USA

ISBN: 979-8-9949894-0-1

This book was created to support environmental education, stewardship, and family learning. While it references real places and concepts, the content is educational in nature and intended for children and families.

Printed in the United States of America

The Place We Call Home

Raising "soft citizens" in the Champlain Adirondack Biosphere Reserve

Written and Illustrated by
Allison Perry

Shared Ground Press

For

Mari, Jackson, and Riley; May you never stop traveling and learning.
My dream to become a published author.
The families and educators of the Champlain Adirondack Biosphere Reserve.

Special Thanks

To my husband, Griffin, for supporting my dreams.
My mentor, Professor Emanuel Carter, for believing in my work and providing his never ending support to make it happen.

If your plan is for one year, plant rice.
If your plan is for ten years, plant trees.
If your plan is for 100 years, educate children.

-Confucius

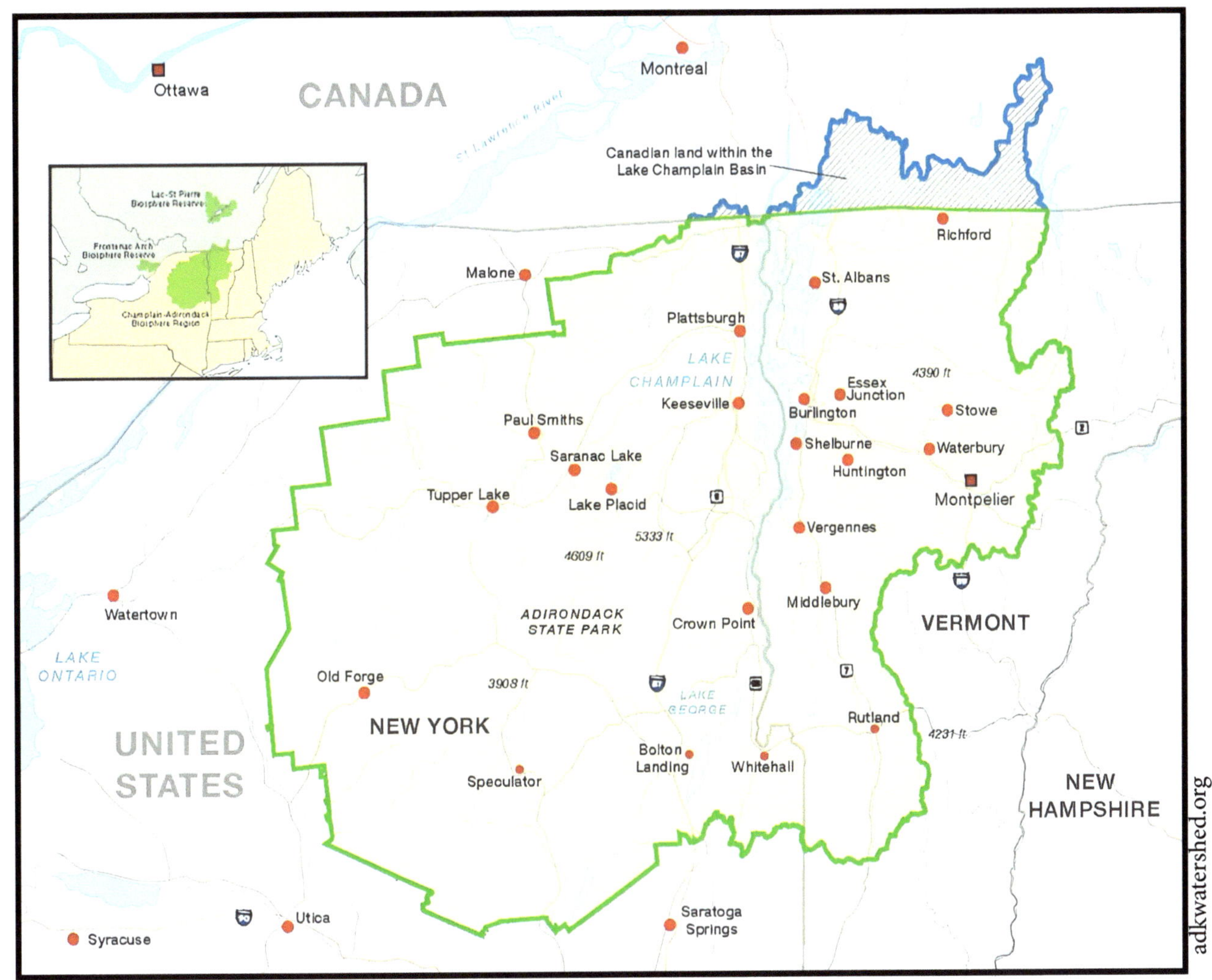

A Note For Parents

The characters in this book are meant to represent the residents that make up the Champlain Adirondack Biosphere Reserve stretching from the Southern Adirondack Mountains to the Green Mountains of Western Vermont.

The story is being told by all the different types of caregivers and educators who have the privledge of reading to and teaching children. I hope the people within the Champlain Adirondack Biosphere Reserve (Network) find some connection to the place they call home and help raise the next generation and all its visitors to understand how special their home really is. **Enjoy!**

To Learn More:
https://champlainvalleynhp.org/heritage/champlain-adirondack-biosphere-reserve/

THE PLACE
WE CALL
HOME

There's a place I know in the Northern Forest. It is unlike any other place in the world.

People visit from all over the globe, but this is where we get to live.

We are lucky. It is special.
It's the place we call home.

Our Home
The Champlain Adirondack Biosphere Reserve

The Place
We Call Home

"How do we know when we get to our home?" asked the oldest girl.

"Ahh," said Papa, nodding. **"There are lots of ways."**

"When you can smell the
pine trees, fresh and strong,
with just one sniff of your nose,"

**... you'll know that
you are home.**

"If the water in your home
comes from Lake Champlain,"

**... you'll know that
you are home.**

"When you see lots of lakes
and streams as you travel
along winding roads,"

**... you'll know that
you are home.**

The Place
We Call
Home

"When people are
working hard in the
villages, the forests,
and the lakes all in one day,"

... you'll know that
you are home.

"If you can see the
mountains of Vermont
or New York,"

**... you'll know that
you are home.**

The Place
We Call Home

"If a loon, or a turtle,
or a fox crosses your path,"

**... you'll know that
you are home.**

The Place
We Call
Home

"When you can celebrate
art made by your neighbors,"

**... you'll know that
you are home.**

"If music and poetry are performed live on a stage throughout the year,"

... you'll know that you are home.

The Place
We Call
Home

"When the forest sings
and the views take your
breath away,"
... you'll know that
you are home.

"Is our home just about the land and the water?" asked the boy.

"It's a big part, but no," Mom said.

She thought and thought of a way to explain.

Fresh
LOCAL
Raspberries

"Do you know how we go to the store and know right away where to find your faaaavorite snacks?"

"Yes!" said the boy.

"They're always next to the cookies, but neeeever past the pickles!"

Mom giggled. **"And do you know how we see Mr. John selling his raspberries at the farmers market every Sunday?"**

"YYYEESSS!" said the boy.

"Mr. John has the sweetest raspberries!"

"He sure does," Mom smiled.

"Well — that's home."

"Home is the people and the living things here, from the rocks, to the lakes, to the rain, to us."

"Home is where our biggest memories are made.

All of these things together are part of our biosphere reserve."

"Without the people and places around us, home wouldn't quiiiite feel like home.

And without people working to care for one another and the world around them, there couldn't be a biosphere reserve."

"Not all of our neighbors are friendly or helpful," mom said.

"But they are all important. And we are a part of their home, too."

"Are there rules?"
questioned the boy.

"Oh yes!!" said Dad.

**"The rules are simple,
but they are very important."**

Leave every place cleaner than you found it. We make the trash, but nature cannot throw it away for us.

Follow the paths made for humans. There is a place for all of us to walk.

Leave animals and their homes alone. There is space for you and space for them, too.

Spread kindness when you can. Happy neighbors make our home a happier place to live.

The Place We Call Home

"Do we live in the only one?"

Asked the girls to their father.

"**No!**" Their dad explained.

"There are over 700 biosphere reserves around the world and more are added all the time."

"They all have the same rules, but none of them look the same.

Each one is special to the people, plants, and animals that call them home."

The Place
We Call Home

“But Dad” said the girl
with a thinking face.

**“What is a
biiii-oh-sss-fere re-WHAT!?”**

Dad chuckled.
"That is a big word!

B-I-O-S-P-H-E-R-E _ R-E-S-E-R-V-E

It's a big place where people live, stretching to the horizon in every direction.

It's a place where people learn, explore, work, and visit."

"But it's also a place where people take care of one another and the land around them.

Biosphere reserves are always learning how people and nature can live best together."

The Place
We Call Home

**"But I'm only a kid, papa,
do I matter in a biosphere
reserve?"** asked the young girl.

**"Kids who live in a biosphere
reserve can grow up to love it,
protect it, and thrive in it"**,
her dad explained proudly.

"The choices you make matter."

"But what can we do?" asked the grandchildren to their grandmother.

"So many things," said Grandma. **"So many things."**

"You can pick up trash and reuse what you have. You'll surely make the turtles smile.

You can play in the woods and fall in love with nature. You can talk to the trees you'll help the forest grow.

You can build a bathouse to bring balance to the things with wings."

The children had asked enough questions for one night. They laid down their heads to think about all they had learned.

As their eyes grew heavy and their thoughts slowed, they fell asleep and started to dream.

They dreamt that they were
part of something bigger.

They dreamt that they were
connected to the creatures
of the forest.

They talked for days about
all the things that made them happy.

“Growing old makes me
the happiest tree I can be.

The older I grow, the more
I can help.

When I finally fall, I like
to stay right where I land.

There, I make homes for others,
clean the air, and keep the forest
safe from fire.”

"Thank you so much
for throwing away
your plastic straw!

Straws that don't get thrown away end up in my water, and it really hurts to get one stuck up your nose!

Have you ever had to pull a straw out of your nose?

YYEEOOWWCH!"

"I just love a good scrub, don't you?" Boomed the moose.

"A scrub is where small trees and bushes grow where I can find food and be safe from wind and sun. A good scrub makes me one happy moose!"

"You know we're pals,
you and me," claimed the fox.

"You share your home
with me, and I help keep
the rodent numbers down.
We take care of each other."

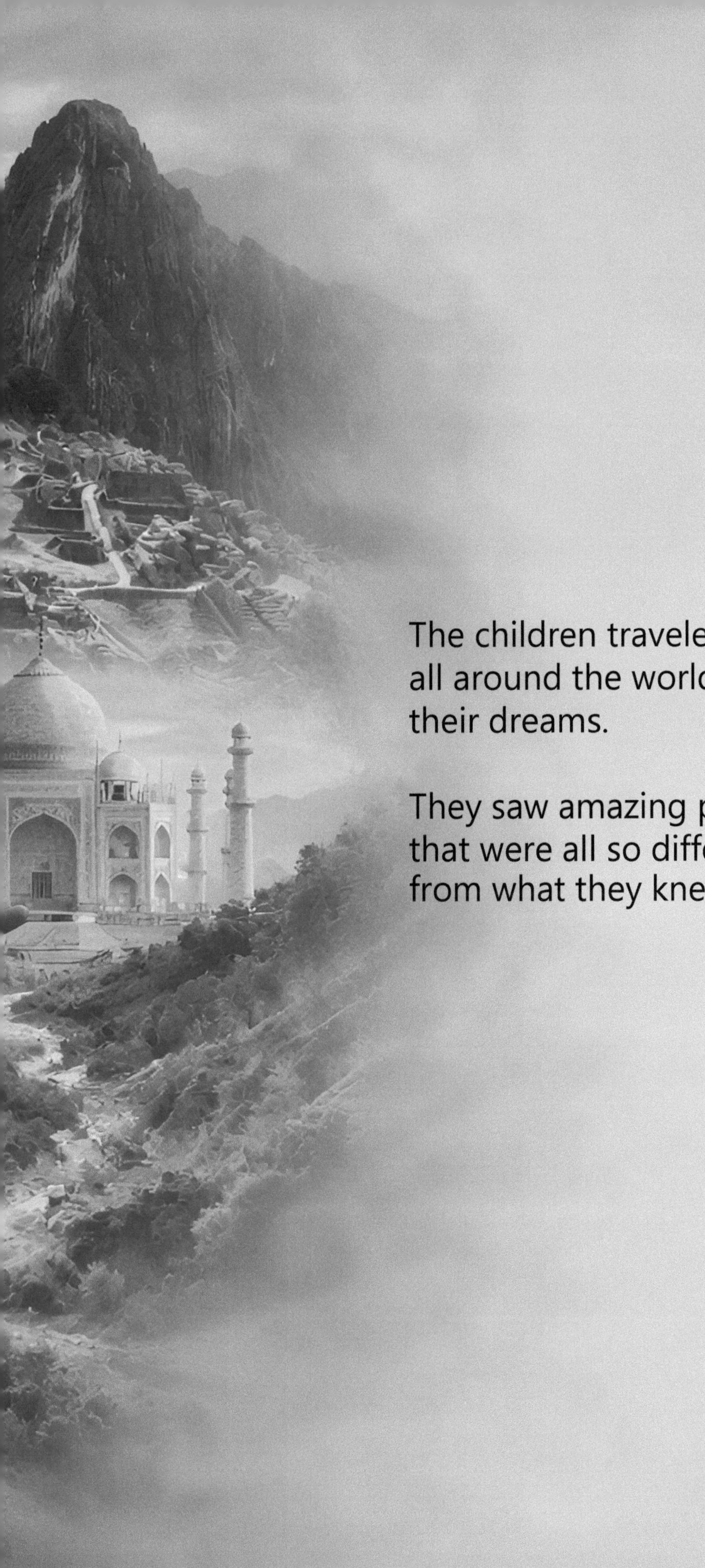

The children traveled
all around the world in
their dreams.

They saw amazing places
that were all so different
from what they knew.

But when their travels were over, they did not need to be told when they were home.

They smelled the trees.
They drank the water.
They listened to the sounds.
and they saw their neighbors.

No... they did not need to be told when they were home.

They just knew.

"Did you know, Mom, that biosphere reserves are so important? Dad, make sure you throw away your wrapper we don't want a fox to choke on it!" chattered the young boy.

"That's very responsible," his mother claimed with a smile. **"I'm so proud of you!"**

"Of course," beamed the boy. **"It's my job. It's everyone's job. We're so lucky to live here. I will take care of our community because it's the place we call home!"**

OUR HOME

The Champlain Adirondack Biosphere Reserve

Educator Note: What Is a UNESCO Biosphere Reserve?

A UNESCO Biosphere Reserve is a special place that has been designated by the United Nations Educational, Scientific, and Cultural Organization (UNESCO) for exemplary efforts to live respectfully with nature. These are places where humans and ecosystems not just live together but thrive, despite one another's influence. In these places, you will find an adbundance of wildlife living among people, their homes, and educational institutions all sharing the same space in a respectful way while educating the community and their visitors about the ecosystems that thrive within it.

Biosphere reserves are not parks set aside from people but rather living landsacpes that embrace towns, farms, forests, waterways, wildlife, and cultures. Each biosphere reserve follows the same guiding ideas that people and nature are strongest when they thrive together. In these shared landscapes, humans and nature have learned to inegreate themselves in a way that should be celebrated and could serve as model places for other communities around the world.

While no biosphere reserves look the same, they are all guided by three shared goals:

1. conservation
2. learning
3. community

The Champlain Adirondack Biosphere Reserve

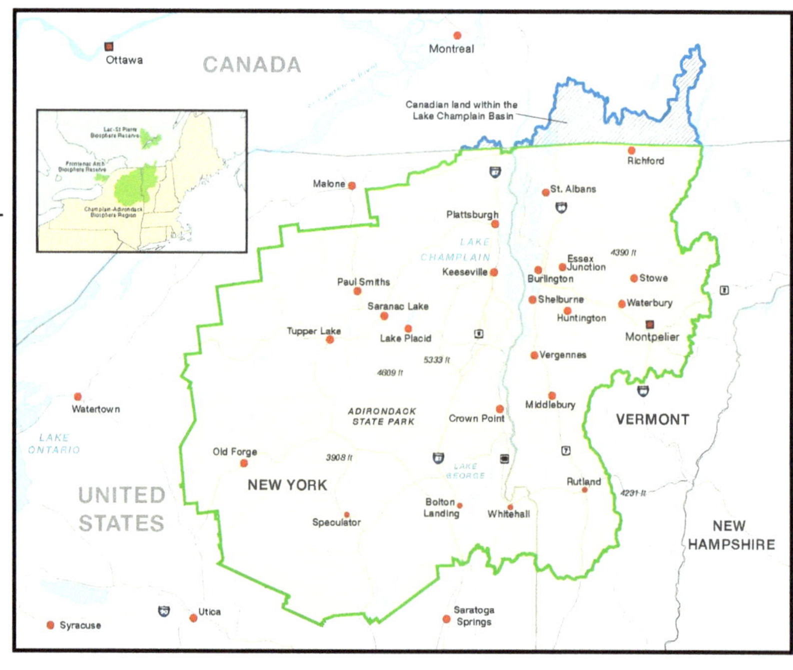

The Champlain Adirondack Biosphere Reserve is a UNESCO-designated region since 1989, located in northeastern New York and western Vermont. It includes mountains, forests, rivers, farms, villages, and Lake Champlain, along with the people who call this place home.

This biosphere reserve recognizes that clean water, healthy forests, local food systems, culture, and strong communities are all connected. Often referred to as "CABN" (Champlain Adirondack Biosphere Network) the reserve makes up around seven million acres of land including extensive coniferous and deciduous forests as well as large numbers of lakes and freshwater wetlands. CABN is one of the largest biosphere reserves around the globe, inhabited by more than 30,000 people and is within one days drive for 60 million people living in the United States and Canada.

A Note to Families

Caring for the world does not begin with big gestures. It begins at home. Children learn how to care for the land, for animals, and for one another by watching the adults around them. When we slow down, notice our surroundings, and treat our shared spaces with respect, children learn to do the same. This is how we raise "soft citizens". Children who grow up with empathy, responsibility, and a quiet understanding that they are part of something larger than themselves. Being a steward of the land does not require perfection or expertise. It grows from small, everyday moments:

- **Picking up a piece of trash together.**
- **Waving hello to a neighbor or holding the door for a stranger.**
- **Staying on a trails made for humans to protect plants and animals.**
- **Thanking the people who grow our food, care for our parks, or clean our spaces.**
- **Turning off lights, saving water, and reusing what we have.**

These moments may seem simple, but they do matter. They teach children that care is a practice, not a rule. Families can also create opportunities for stewardship by inviting children to participate in:

- **Gardening, even in a small space.**
- **Walking instead of driving to close destinations when it's possible.**
- **Visiting local farms, musuems, forests, lakes, or libraries.**
- **Talking about where water comes from and where waste goes.**
- **Encouraging curiosity about the natural world and finding the answers to the questions they have together.**

Most importantly, children need to see their adults leading by example. When we treat the land and our neighbors with kindness, children learn that stewardship is not something we are told to do, but rather, it is something we choose to do. Raising "soft citizens" means raising children who are gentle with the places they love, thoughtful in their choices, and confident that their actions matter. These children grow into adults who care for their communities, their environment, and each other.

Conversation Starters & Activities

What makes our home special?
Who are the human and non-human neighbors where we live?
What rules do you think help keep our shared places healthy and safe?
When we flush our toilets, where do you think our waste goes?
Where do you think our water comes from when turn on the sink?
Where did the food on our plate come from? How did it get there?

"The Place We Call Home" is intended to support place-based learning and spark conversations about stewardship, responsibility, and belonging, beginning with the landscapes children know best. **We hope The Place We Call Home opens the door to conversations, questions, and shared experiences that help families grow together—rooted in care for the world we all share.**

Family Stewardship Checklist

Small actions. Shared responsibility. Caring for the place we call home.

At Home

_______ Turn off lights when leaving a room
_______ Use water thoughtfully (shorter showers, turn off the tap)
_______ Reuse bags, containers, and paper when possible
_______ Sort recycling and trash together
_______ Talk about where food, water, and energy come from

Outdoors

_______ Stay on trails to protect plants and animals
_______ Pick up litter—even if it isn't yours
(keep a pair of gloves or extra trash bag handy when adventuring)
_______ Leave rocks, plants, and animals where they belong
_______ Walk, bike, or explore nearby places when possible
_______ Notice wildlife and talk about how they live

Water & Wildlife Care

_______ Keep trash out of lakes, streams, and drains
_______ Use reusable water bottles and lunch containers
_______ Talk about how animals use water and land
_______ Respect nests, dens, and animal homes
_______ Learn the names of a few local plants or animals

Community Care

_______ Be kind to neighbors and visitors
_______ Thank people who care for shared spaces (janitorial, sanitation, construction)
_______ Support local farms, markets, and businesses
_______ Learn about the land's history and people who live there
_______ Share what you know about caring for your home

Raising "Soft Citizens"

_______ Model kindness toward people and nature
_______ Invite questions and curiosity
_______ Celebrate effort, not perfection
_______ Make stewardship part of everyday life
_______ Talk with (and around) your kids about the things happening in the community.

Remember: small choices add up! Practice, not perfection!

Champlain Adirondack Exploration Bucket List

A chance to explore, practice, learn, and get curious!

Water Wonders

______ Paddle, skip stones, spot ducks & sailboats as you watch the water in *Lake Champlain.*
____ __ *Valcour Island:* A boat only adventure that feels like a secret hideout.
____ __ Catch the sunset at *Charlotte Beach* with a view of the Adirondack Mountains across the lake.
______ *Burlington Waterfront Park*: Bike paths, playgrounds, and room to run with a view of the lake!
______ Swim, boat, or explore *Lake George.*
______ Camp and catch sunsets in *Saranac Lake.*
______ Dine on the water, shop in the villages, and have so much fun exploring *Lake Placid.*

Easy Nature Adventures (Big wows, little legs)

______ *Ausable Chasm* - Bridges, waterfalls, & rock walls carved by rushing water.
______ *Hurricane Mountain Fire Tower* - a short hike to a tower with a "you can see forever" view
______ *Point Au Roche State Park* - Nature trails, beaches, and picnic spots perfect for families.

Farms & Friendly Animals

____ *Shelburne Farms* - cows, horses, barns, hikes, and hands on learning about land and food!
____ *Misty Knoll Farm* - Pasture raised animals and a farm store kids love to explore.
____ *Harmony Hills Farm* - Alpacas, farm fun, and lots of smiles
____ *North Country Creamery* - Dairy farm views and delicious local products.

Ice Cream Stops (science and smiles)

____ *Adirondack Creamery* (https://adirondackcreamery.com/)
____ *Creemee Stand* (Vermont's iconic soft serve)
____ *Speculator Creamery* (Speculator, New York)
____ *Skyline Ice Cream* (Tupper Lake)
____ *Sisters of Anarchy Ice Cream* (Vermont)
____ Ben and Jerrys Factory Tour (Vermont)

Museums to explore, Like No Other!

____ *The Wild Center* - Tupper Lake
____ *The Adirondack Experience at Blue Mountain Lake*
____ *ECHO - Leahy Center for Lake Champlain*

This list is only a start! What else did you find!?
Tell me: https://allietheauthor.carrd.co/

Defining "Soft Citizenship"

The term citizen is commonly defined as a person who belongs to a government or place, often understood through borders, taxes, and political systems—structures created by humans to impose order on a world that does not recognize those lines. Nature neither acknowledges nor consents to the boundaries we draw, yet our definition of citizenship has largely ignored our reciprocal relationship with the land itself. I believe an essential dimension is missing from this conversation: **what I call "soft citizenship".**

A soft citizen is someone who understands their belonging not only to a government, but to the land they inhabit—recognizing stewardship of that place as an inherent responsibility rather than an optional act. We are all citizens of this planet, dependent on its forests, waters, and ecosystems for survival. When we degrade the land, we pay a real cost in the form of collective health, resilience, and well-being. Raising "**soft citizens",** particularly within biosphere reserves, means instilling care for place and community as a foundational value, helping future generations live in relationship with the land in ways that allow both people and ecosystems to thrive for years to come.

Family Promise

We promise to care for our home—
the land, the water, the people, and the living things—
by making thoughtful choices and helping one another
when we can.

Signed: ____________________________

Date: ____________________________

About the Author

Allison Perry is a writer, designer, and advocate for place-based education. She lives in Central New York with her family and holds a master's degree in Mental Health Counseling with a specialization in childhood play therapy (2012), as well as a master's degree in Landscape Architecture (2024).

She wrote The Place We Call Home to address a gap in resources for children and families—one that connects emotional development, environmental stewardship, and a sense of belonging. Through her work, Allison seeks to bring people, nature, and education together in meaningful and lasting ways.

Allison hopes that this book will be the first in a series of books about Biosphere Reserves around the world.

www.ingramcontent.com/pod-product-compliance
Ingram Content Group UK Ltd.
Pitfield, Milton Keynes, MK11 3LW, UK
UKHW060117300726
14090UKWH00002B/250

* 9 7 9 8 9 9 4 9 8 9 4 0 1 *